PEOPLE
ONE OUGHT
TO KNOW

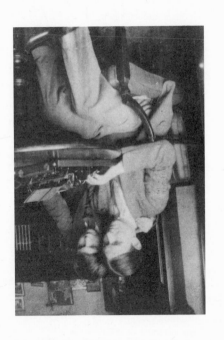

PEOPLE ONE OUGHT TO KNOW

By
Christopher Isherwood

Illustrations by
Sylvain Mangeot

DOUBLEDAY & COMPANY, INC.
GARDEN CITY, NEW YORK
1982

CHRISTOPHER ISHERWOOD is a distinguished writer. Born in Cheshire, England, the son of an army officer, Mr. Isherwood spent much of his childhood traveling around with his father's regiment. He attended Repton School and Cambridge and, after working for André Mangeot, studied medicine briefly. Mr. Isherwood lived in Germany for four years with his friend and fellow poet W. H. Auden, and then traveled extensively throughout Europe and China, finally coming to the United States in 1939 where he became an American citizen in 1946. Mr. Isherwood has worked as an editor and scriptwriter and is the author of many novels, plays, travel diaries, articles, poems, stories (including "The Berlin Stories" from which the movie *Cabaret* was made) and an autobiography, *Lions and Shadows*. Mr. Isherwood lives in Santa Monica, California.

SYLVAIN MANGEOT was born in London, England, in 1913. He was a King's Scholar at Westminster School and gained an honors degree in modern languages at Oxford University. After completing the illustrations for *People One Ought to Know* as a young boy, he went on to distinguish himself in a variety of journalistic fields. After serving as a Foreign Office press officer, then as deputy head of the French Section of the Political Intelligence Department, he became the first diplomatic correspondent for the Reuter news service. Later he was an editor for *Picture Post* and the *News Chronicle,* and for twenty years before his sudden death in 1978 he was a greatly respected commentator for the Overseas Broadcasting Department of the BBC. Mr. Mangeot, also author of the book *The Adventures of a Manchurian,* was a world traveler and had a keen interest in sports. He was a first-class fisherman and cook, greatly respected in his work, and loved by his wide circle of friends.

Library of Congress Catalog Card Number 81–43424
ISBN: 0-385-17536-1

INTRODUCTION

It has long been considered that *All the Conspirators,* published in 1928, was Christopher Isherwood's first book, but this is not strictly true.

The present volume is the result of a chance series of events which, in 1925, brought together a most unlikely artistic combination. My uncle, Sylvain Mangeot, was at that time eleven years old, while the now long established literary exile Christopher Isherwood was twice that age and working in our London home as secretary to my grandfather, a professional violinist.

The bohemian disorder of the Mangeot ("Cheuret") household, with which Christopher felt so instantly at one, is described vividly in Chapter Four of *Lions and Shadows,* his early volume of autobiography. The Cheuret veil was a pretty thin and transparent one, and to call that work fiction is to do an injustice to the disarmingly accurate portraits which certain members of my family have been trying to live down ever since. My father "Jean," for example, must have found Christopher's first impression that he was "less intelligent and more English" than his brother rather disconcerting—both equal heresies when you live under so Francophile a roof.

Christopher worked in the mews house at Cresswell Place for about a year and quickly became one of the family. He fell in love with all its members and they, in turn, looked upon him as the elder brother and son he longed to be. It was, in a sense, from the former role that *People One Ought to Know* grew, although tracing the book's progression from initial inspiration to completed project is really a glimpse into the impulsiveness of childhood.

The project began when Sylvain returned from a shopping expedition toward the end of one school holiday with the catalyst. Some loose-leaf sheets of high-quality handmade paper had caught his eye— the kind of paper one hesitates to mark without a convenient masterpiece in mind. Clearly, with only a matter of days to the new term, a sense of desperate urgency fired the creative muse.

Christopher mentions in *Lions and Shadows* that "Edouard" (Sylvain) was "clever at making little drawings and writing verses." In this instance, Sylvain began by humanizing a couple of delightfully comic animal sketches—both by the inventive regalia in which they were clad and by some short accompanying doggerel rhymes. Pleased with the drawings but dissatisfied with the comparative merit of his own poetry, Sylvain philosophically decided that Christopher might be able to do better.

I'm not certain that, having completed the verse that would keep "The Cormorant" company, Christopher quite appreciated his fellow artist's prolific intentions: namely, that every side of the freshly sliced paper should have its own rhyme to partner the feverishly multiplying animals; that the result should be bound and signed by "the authors"; and, in short, that the gestation period and birth pangs were to take altogether less than a week. Even for a slim volume, this still seems an incredible achievement given the consistent freshness and spontaneity throughout.

In *Lions and Shadows*, Christopher also murmurs briefly about lack of spare time; either things improved or, as I suspect, he used his own time to get the verses written. Every mad couplet still preserves the happiness and enjoyment of that youthful idyllic interlude, the empathy with drawings that were entirely lacking in self-consciousness and therefore so perfectly right; and, most of all, the deep love for the temporary home and family where, by sheer chance, he found himself.

Andrew Mangeot

CROCODILE

Here Mr. Z——, a crocodile,
Boards the boat-train for Carlisle.
Living is cheap there, that's the reason
So many are visiting it this season.
The careless shopmen leave large chops
Hanging outside the butchers' shops,
And if you're clever, you can lunch,
Without paying, off a bunch
Of liver sausages, or maybe
A stupid nursemaid's left a baby
Unprotected in its pram—
(Babies are very nice with ham)—
Hence the sleek and jolly smile
On the face of this crocodile.

RABBIT

The funny appearance of this rabbit
Was caused by its disgusting habit
Of eating porridge with its tea.
It was a case of obstinacy—
His friends all told him it was risky.
But he said, "I'm as right as whisky;
I've got that splendid Kruschen feeling*
I can jump higher than the ceiling."
They shook their heads. He only sneered,
"You could be like me if you dared,
As strong and healthy. . . ."
                    Three weeks sped.
The doctor says he'll soon be dead.
He won't be sorry to reach the grave—
Five times a day he has to shave
These horrible whiskers that make him sneeze—
They're the nastiest part of his disease.

* "that Kruschen feeling": meaning with verve and energy. From an
advertisement for Kruschen Salts, c. 1925.

SHARK

A common error about the shark
Is that its bite's worse than its bark.
But, as I have too often found,
The truth is just the other way round—
Imagine a giant knife and fork
Scratching a plate the size of New York,
Or the way a slate pencil squeaks and rubs
When the slate is bigger than Wormwood Scrubs,
Or an organ played by paralyzed cats,
Or a gong being struck with cricket bats
By a party of drunk and angry bears;
Imagine an elephant in tears,
Imagine me singing the whole of *Tannhäuser,*
And you get some idea of the wonderful noise a
Shark can make when it's really cross
To hear that Australia won the toss.

FARMER STOAT

Every Thursday, Farmer Stoat
Puts on his long-tailed green frock-coat,
His blue hat, and his golden breeches
And goes to town to sell his peaches.
     The Farmer is a wicked cheat—
     His peaches are no good to eat,
     They're hard as wood and dry as straw,
     Maggots are swarming in the core,
     But all the same, he sells them fast;
     Soon he is handing out the last.
     Showing his teeth, he tells the mice,
     "You'd better buy, they're very nice."
     The poor mice shiver in their shoes—
     Not one of them would dare refuse.
     They know what happens if you do
     And the Farmer catches you
     After dark, in some quiet lane
     As he's driving home again.
But soon I hope that that good soul,
Parson Badger, takes a stroll
Through the market with his stick
And beats the Farmer till he's sick.
It's about time that someone teaches
We're tired of him and his bad peaches.

SNAKE

This is an ordinary kind of snake.
You may find one if you shake
Almost any pillow or mat,
Or the gardener's dirty old straw hat,
Or a fur rug that you've kept a cat on.
He looks so floppy because he's been sat on;
But beware—a nip from the creature's molars
Will give you an ache like four steam-rollers.
However, if a person handles
Him kindly and feeds him on chopped candles,
He will be gentle as a dove
And show an almost filial love.

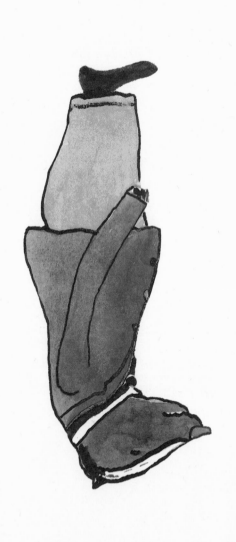

BADGER

The only fault I find with badgers
Is that they're such appalling cadgers.
If you ask one out to dine
He'll want a dozen of your wine
To take home. If he likes your prints
He'll bother you with clumsy hints:
"I say, who's that picture by? . . .
It's my birthday next July. . . ."
Once, one asked me for my car—
This was going rather far—
So I said, "Wouldn't you rather
Take this ring? It belonged to my father;
It's set with diamonds." Calm and bland,
He thanked me and held out his hand.
I had an apoplectic fit:
The Badger walked away with it.

BEAR

No wonder this bear looks rather wild,
For the idiotic child
Has just smoked eight cigars from Havana,
Some hay wrapped up in an old banana,
Ten pipes and a chocolate cigarette.
They've called the parson and the vet.
The vet is sharpening his shears,
The parson's reading funeral prayers.
At half past nine they'll operate.
The vet says it'll be too late.
But "Never mind," is the parson's reply,
"he'll be happy beyond the sky."
This comforts them, for no one cares
What happens to foolish teddy-bears.

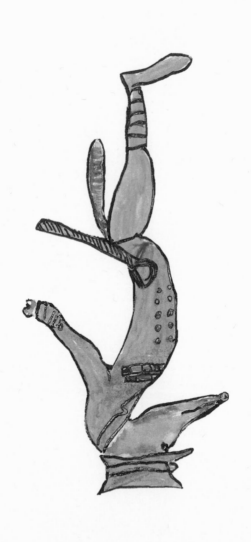

WEASEL KING

When I am old and feeble grown
And children ask me who I've known
Among the novelists and peers
And great men of my early years,
I shall reply, with haughty look,
"I've never met an earl or duke
Nor a marquis, but I'll sing
About my friend the Weasel King."
His Majesty was small but vicious—
He thought a rabbit's ear delicious
To eat for breakfast, and could bite
Through leather or through vulcanite.
If he ever saw a stoat
He jumped and caught it by the throat.
He led his people into battle
And cut the badgers down like cattle.
Blood was his favourite drink, then cider,
He was no temperance-pledge abider.
His scream was louder than ten geese,
When angry;

         But in times of peace,

He passed a life of ease and culture
With his favourite pet, a vulture.
He didn't live—quite the contrary—
In a palace like George and Mary.
He scorned vast throne-rooms, and instead
Spent nearly all the day in bed.
Just after tea-time he'd begin
To practice on his violin—
He had composed a fine lament
On one note, for this instrument—
And when the music soothed his soul,
He'd take his pipe and fill the bowl
And light it up, and call for lamps,
Chatting of heraldry and stamps.
And once, after a solemn feast,
He rose and pinned upon my breast
A cross awarded for great merit—
The Order of the Woollen Ferret.
So that is why I always sing,
"God bless our gracious Weasel King."

HIPPO

The Hoover Hippo's vacuum jaw
Absorbed into his hungry maw
All kinds of food, from iron to suet.
Most wonderful how he could do it—
He swallowed clocks and cannon-balls
Twice nightly at the music halls.
The people clapped and shouted loud,
He was the idol of the crowd;
Until, on an unlucky day,
A spy of the R.S.P.C.A.*
Found him out and had him sued
And sentenced to penal servitude.

* Royal Society for Prevention of Cruelty to Animals

GIRAFFE

Ill-mannered boys perhaps may laugh
At the curious spots on this giraffe.
"What are they for?" you ask. Well, I
Will tell you; each is a bull's-eye
And has afforded constant practice
To many marksmen. For the fact is,
During the War, this creature was mascot
To a regiment quartered at Ascot,
And every morning they would shoot
All over it, from head to foot;
Such was the toughness of its skin
That not one bullet entered in.
Now that you've heard this, you'll at least
Not laugh at the patriotic beast.

ADMIRAL DUCK

Admiral Duck is so conceited,
His navy always gets defeated.
He thinks the enemy are fools
Because they don't obey the rules
He's set down in volume four
Of his book: *The Tactics of Naval War*.
First he was beaten by the rats;
They blew his boats into cocked hats.
The dab-chicks gave him some nasty knocks;
And now the newts, in a cigarette-box
Fitted up with a paper sail,
Have made the Admiral turn tail.
Thinking of this last reverse,
He begins to swear and curse
As he waddles the deck; but already he plots
To capture some of the model yachts
On the Round Pond, and with these
To become the Monarch of the Seas.

CORMORANT

The common cormorant (or shag)
Lays eggs inside a paper bag.
You follow the idea, no doubt?
It's to keep the lightning out.

But what these unobservant birds
Have never thought of, is that herds
Of wandering bears might come with buns
And steal the bags to hold the crumbs.

BUTTERFLY

The Patchwork Admiral Butterfly
Likes to find some warm and dry
Parlour or drawing-room, and there
Settle. It hates the open air.
It does not waste its youthful powers
Fluttering over pretty flowers.
It would far prefer to rove
Round a gas-fire or a stove.
This may be why, as I am told,
Some live to be seventy-five years old.

BAT

No, reader, this is not a mouse,
Nor a slow-worm, nor a louse,
Nor a conjurer at a fair,
Producing things out of the air,
Nor one of those performing snails
Doing an Eastern dance with veils.
This is just a simple bat—
Really nothing to laugh at.

FROG

This tiresome frog is making a fuss—
He wants to go for a trip on a bus.
We've all been persuading him
To give up this foolish whim.
We've offered him every kind of treat
If he won't—nice things to eat,
A sugar parrot, a chocolate mouse,
High tea at Lyons Corner House;
Or a real live monkey for a pet,
Or gallery seats at *No, No, Nanette,*
Or a velvet pincushion shaped like a heart,
Or a ride in the greengrocer's cart,
In a cab, in a taxi—we've tried them all.
But he answers, "It *must* be a General.
It *must* be Number Seventy-three.
And I *must* get back here late for tea."
What can one do with such a child?
I think his parents are far too mild.

HARE

A ballet-dancer was Miss Hare—
Her attitudes made people stare,
Until she caught her face a crack
Doing a high kick round in back
While impersonating Cupid.
Since then, she's been a trifle stupid.
Out there in the street you may
See her almost any day,
Wandering with hands tightly clasped
In front of her. I've often gasped
To watch the vague and dreamy way
She steps before a cart or dray,
In spite of the drivers' objurgations
And the things they say about her relations.

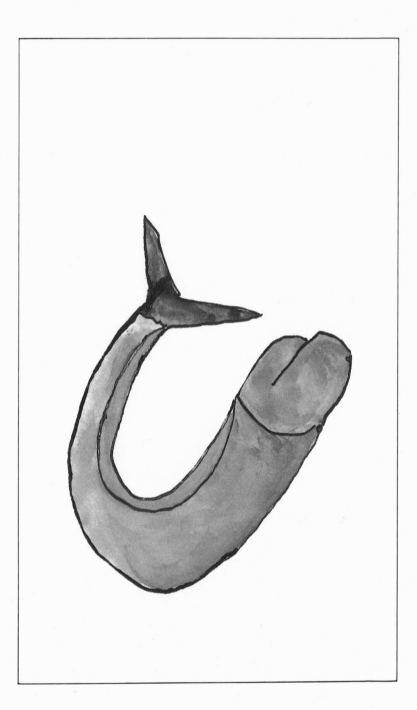

WHALE

He's trying desperately, this whale,
To put his head beneath his tail.
He's frightened because someone's told
Him that his stomach's turning gold—
And as you know, with whales and weasels,
When one turns gold, he's got the measles.
As a matter of fact, our friend has not.
He's only slipped on a treacle-pot
Dropped from the deck of a submarine
By the cabin-boy, who was feeling green.

SIEGFRIED

Siegfried's proud of his new blazer—
Having just managed to raise a
First Eleven cap for cricket.
(Siegfried stands behind the wicket.)
Certain games masters may feel
Prejudice against a seal
Playing for one of our Public Schools.
But if you look in Wisden's rules,
You won't find it forbidden, ever.
Besides, Siegfried is so clever
At stumping people with his fin
That they had to let him in.
But it's amazing what spite can
Be shown by sportsmen. There's a plan
That poor Siegfried shan't appear
In the team photograph this year.

PARROT

"I don't know how I'd stand the strain,"
Said a parrot we met once in the train,
"Of being cooped up day after day
And shouting, 'Pretty Poll!'; 'Hip hooray!';
'Chawley!' and 'Damn you' and 'Mind your eye!'
Hanging in that conservatory,
While silly people drink their tea
And make idiotic remarks to me—
If it wasn't that I sometimes get
Out to the country with a net.
Then I'm happy. No doubt you've guessed
I'm an ardent lepidopterist.
At home, I should think that I have quite
Four thousand examples of Cabbage White.
I can collect no other kind,
For unfortunately, I'm colour-blind."

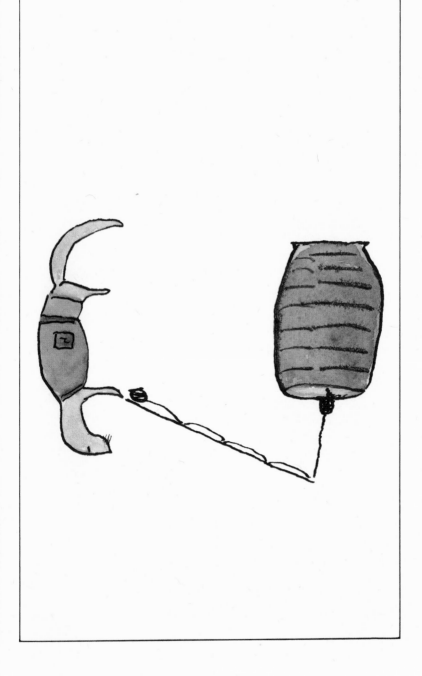

FERRETS

Why do ferrets fish in tubs
With brand-new rods and worms and grubs?
Really, there's something of the mystic
About them, they're so optimistic.
From twelve inches of clear water
They expect to find they've caught a
Fish, at least, if not a trout.
And if they got a salmon out,
Their ignorance of Nature's such,
It would not surprise them much.

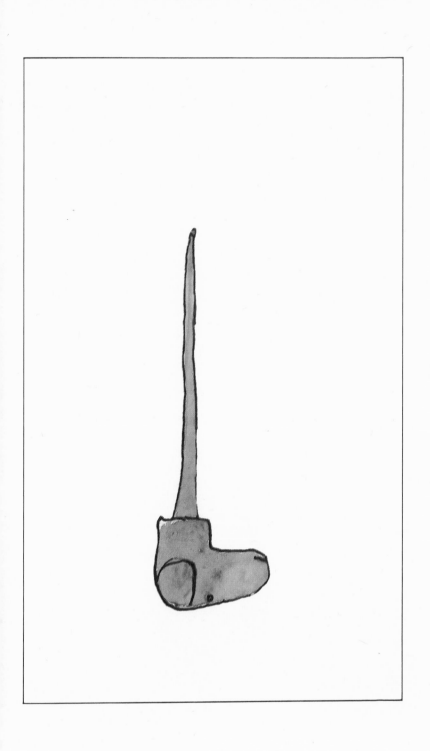

HOUND

The wondrous beauty of this hound
Was famed throughout the country round.
And carvers, after it was dead,
Made a model of its head
Into a stick to take out walking.

One day, the wooden head began talking
It recited the multiplication tables
Till they locked it in the stables,
Where it bit the gardener's daughter.

I don't know really that I ought to
Accept this tale as perfectly true.
I heard it from someone in the zoo.

CAMEL

"I confess," said the camel, "I sometimes wish
My hump wasn't shaped like a pudding-dish.
We might have been fitted with something pretty—
Like the Turkish mosque at the old white city;
Or why not a statue or a flower,
Or a helmet and crest or a tree, or a tower
Carved with scenes from some classical story, all
In marble and gold, like the Albert Memorial?"

"Well, well," I said mildly, "there's no deciding—
But a tree'd be rather a nuisance when riding."

SQUIRREL

This squirrel, although so young and small,
Doesn't live in a tree at all.
One day he left the woods for the town
And now he's climbing up and down
The telegraph-pole outside our house.

He hears us grumble, he hears us grouse,
He hears us gnash and rage and curse,
He hears us quarrel; and, what's worse,
He sometimes jumps on the sill and pokes
His head inside and hears our jokes.

Oh, if that squirrel ever returns
To his native forests, my cheek burns
To think of the tales he'll spread about—
It'll make his parents' fur drop out.

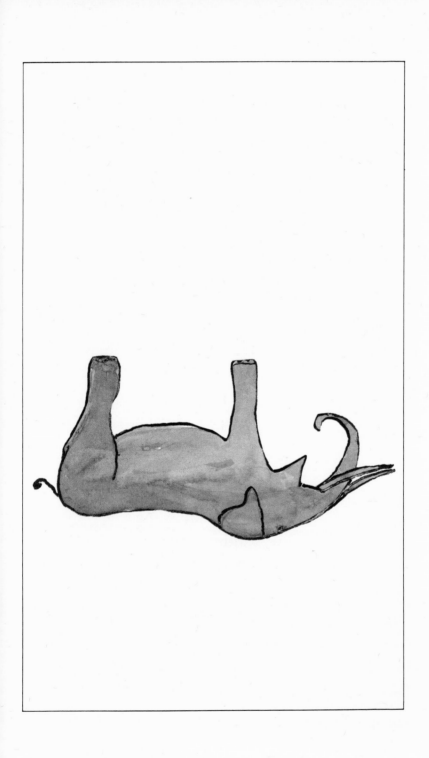

ELEPHANT

Don't argue with an elephant.
It's no use, for you simply can't
Convince any of these stupid creatures;
Just look at the brute's stolid features—
Not a gleam of common sense.
In fact, the elephant's so dense
That if you tell him white is white,
And go on saying so all night,
And prove it with a piece of string
And three rulers, if you bring
Learned books on Maths and Stinks—
Still he only sits and blinks
And murmurs, "Oh yes, yes . . . I've seen
Your arguments; but white is green."

OSTRICH

This ostrich is a first-class runner.
Only just last year he won a
Box of paints and a silver jar
In a race against a motor-car.
His methods of training are rather weird.
At half past six, he has prepared
A porridge of oats and tar and stout.
After this, he walks about
Dragging an iron ball on a chain.
At a quarter to one, he eats again—
This time, it is boiling glue and tacks.
Then the trainer comes and gives him whacks
With a sledge-hammer upon the legs.
Then they fix his feet to the boards with pegs
And he flaps his wings till he lifts up the floor.
Then they stand him against the door
And slam it on him to make him thin.
And at nine o'clock he dines off gin.
These are things any boy can do.
But I'd leave out the tar, if I were you.

DOE

Here is Titus, our pet doe,
The biggest hypocrite I know.
When visitors come to the house,
He's quiet and gentle as a mouse.
They say, "Oh, the pretty lamb,
Would he like some bread and jam?"
And the artful creature stands
And lets them feed him from their hands.
Maiden ladies stroke his ears
And murmur, practically in tears,
"Look at his great wistful eyes. . . ."

They would get a slight surprise
If they saw him bite the cook.
As for those great eyes—well, look
A little closer, and you'll see
That one of them is black. That's me.
I hit him with a rolling pin
To stop him hacking at my shin.
Yesterday he killed a cat,
And ate the mutton, lean and fat,
And smashed the china in the sink.
Why we keep him, I can't think—
Except that it's sometimes amusing
To hear the visitors enthusing.

SNAIL

The snail has a telephone and bell
Fitted up inside his shell.
He says the thing's a perfect pest:
"When I come out to digest
For forty seconds in the sun,
The bell rings, and in I run.
But usually, it's just a call,
Or: 'Is that Harrods?', 'Is that Alice?',
'Is that George at Buckingham Palace?'
I never have a wink of slumber—
Somebody always gets my number."

HORSEY

Horsey in his youth loved Footer.
Here he is, about to shoot a
Goal for Manchester United—
Crowds of frantically excited
Miners, bank-clerks, dukes and earls,
And adoring office-girls
Yell with triumph as their hero
Raises the visitors' score from zero.

CAT AND DOG

Last week, in the High Street, during the fog,
A policeman observed this bright green dog
Wearing a saddle of scarlet leather
And scampering along together
With a mud-covered cat of the usual sort.

The constable wrote a report
To the sergeant, who sent it, with his card,
To Sherlock Holmes at Scotland Yard.

Holmes wrote back: "I shan't waste my time
Explaining such a simple crime,
Committed at your very doors.
The clues point straight to Barkers Stores."

So a hundred policemen dressed in mail
Raided Barkers' during a sale.
They blew their whistles and called out "Stop!"
They arrested everyone in the shop.
They opened parcels and undid cases,
They examined the stock from beans to braces—
Mr. Barker is in tears.
They'll search each shelf if it takes ten years.

Meanwhile, somebody sent to say
Holmes had gone for a holiday.
They wired to him on the Riviera:
"No luck." He wired back: "I don't care a———."

And that's the up-to-the-present history
Of the Mud-Coloured Cat and Green Dog Mystery.